Parallel History

One Period | Global Developments | Side by Side

THE MODERN ⚙ WORLD ⚙

1900 – Now

Alex Woolf

Illustrated by
Victor Beuren

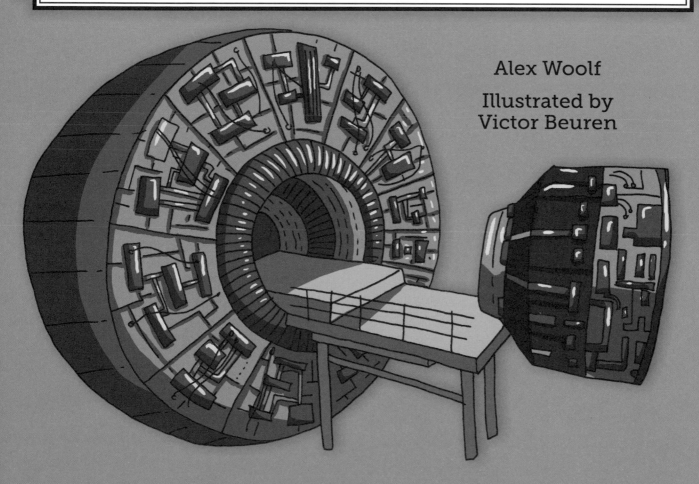

W

FRANKLIN WATTS
LONDON•SYDNEY

Franklin Watts
First published in Great Britain in 2017
by The Watts Publishing Group

Copyright © The Watts Publishing Group 2017

Credits
Artwork by Victor Beuren
Design: Collaborate Agency
Editor: Nicola Edwards

ISBN 978 1 4451 5736 8

Printed in China

Franklin Watts
An imprint of
Hachette Children's Group
Part of The Watts Publishing Group
Carmelite House
50 Victoria Embankment
London EC4Y 0DZ

An Hachette UK Company
www.hachette.co.uk

www.franklinwatts.co.uk

MIX
Paper from
responsible sources
FSC® C104740

⚙ CONTENTS ⚙

☼ INTRODUCTION ☼

Since 1900, the world has undergone many changes. Two global wars shook the existing order. Europe's colonial powers saw their significance decline and their empires disappear, while other nations, such as the USA and China, grew stronger. For much of the later twentieth century, the world divided into two hostile camps during the so-called 'Cold War'.

Colour Key
- Nato
- US Allies
- Warsaw Pact
- USSR Allies
- Neutral territories

During the Cold War, the world was dominated by the superpowers, the USA and the Soviet Union (formed from the old Russian Empire).

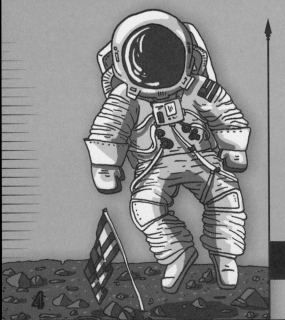

Progress

The modern era has seen some huge technological leaps. The invention of powered flight led to regular air travel for millions. The space programme sent satellites into orbit and probes to other planets. The horse, our means of transport for thousands of years, was replaced by the car. Improved diet and medicine increased average life expectancy by almost 30 years.

In 1969, the first humans walked on the Moon.

Globalisation

Mass media, telecommunications, the Internet and social media all helped spread knowledge and create a more globalised culture. With cheaper travel, increasing numbers moved in search of a better life. Businesses, too, grew more international as it became easier to move money and goods around the world. The trend towards a more interconnected world became known as globalisation.

Women had to fight hard to win the right to vote.

Social media has helped bring people closer together, wherever they live.

Social change

Over time, Western society became more respectful of the rights of ethnic minorities and the LGBTQ+ community. Women fought for and won rights bringing them closer to equality with men. These struggles continue to this day, especially in cultures with more conservative attitudes. Globalisation brought social benefits, but also caused tensions: some resented the arrival of immigrants, and many lost their jobs to workers in countries where wages were lower.

The city of Aleppo, devastated by the civil war in Syria that began in 2011.

Conflict

War became far more deadly during the modern era with the development of tanks, machine guns, poison gas, aerial bombardment, missiles and nuclear weapons. As a result, tens of millions died in the two world wars. There has been no global conflict since 1945, but numerous smaller-scale wars in the Middle East, Africa and southern Asia. The era has also seen a rise in terrorism with extremist groups carrying out mass attacks on innocent people.

☼ THE FIRST WORLD WAR ☼

The 'Great War' began as a European conflict, with Germany, Austria-Hungary and the Ottoman Empire (the Central Powers) on one side, and Britain, France and Russia (the Allies) on the other. But as these powers were empires, the war soon spread to their territories in other parts of the world, making it the first global war. It was also the first 'total war' as nations mobilised their entire populations and all their resources to achieve victory.

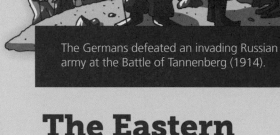

The Germans defeated an invading Russian army at the Battle of Tannenberg (1914).

Soldiers had to survive appalling conditions in the trenches.

The Eastern Front

In eastern Europe, Russia fought Germany and Austria-Hungary (the Central Powers). The war ebbed and flowed with neither side making a decisive breakthrough. A Russian counter-offensive in June 1916 nearly knocked Austria-Hungary out of the war, but exhausted Russia. In 1917 the Russian tsar was overthrown in a revolution, and in March 1918 Russia pulled out of the war.

The Western Front

The Germans fought France and Britain in western Europe. Both sides soon realised that the only way of defending against machine guns and artillery was to dig trenches. For three and a half years the front line barely moved. Attempts were made to break the deadlock using poison gas, flame throwers and tunnelling. Both sides launched major offensives at Verdun and the Somme at a terrible cost in lives and for very little progress.

| Sept 1914 | The start of trench warfare on the Western Front | Battle of the Somme, resulting in more than 1.5 million casualties | Jul – Nov 1916 |

| June 1914 | Assassination of the Austro-Hungarian archduke Franz Ferdinand by a Serbian nationalist sparks World War I. (Austria-Hungary declared war on Serbia, so Russia declared war on Austria-Hungary, so Germany declared war on Russia, so France and Britain declared war on Germany.) |

| Battle of Verdun, with 600,000–976,000 casualties | Feb – Dec 1916 |

The Italians gained little territory but suffered enormous casualties before their defeat in October 1917.

Italy and the Dardanelles

Italy joined the war in May 1915 on the side of the Allies, and fought Austria-Hungary along the Isonzo River. Another front opened in February 1915 when the Allies tried to take control of the sea route to Russia by attacking Turkish forces at Gallipoli in the Dardanelles. The assault was a costly failure for the Allies.

The USA

US president Woodrow Wilson pledged to remain neutral during the war, but increasing attacks on neutral ships in the Atlantic by German submarines led him to change his mind. The USA's entry into the war on the side of the Allies in April 1917 proved decisive. By August 1918 the Central Powers had been thrown on the defensive. Three months later, the war was over.

The sinking of the Lusitania by a German submarine in May 1915 turned public opinion in the USA against Germany.

USA enters the war — *April 1917*	Russia accepts terms of Treaty of Brest-Litovsk, ending Russian involvement in World War I — *3 March 1918*	*1 June 1918* — Start of Battle of Bellau Wood (victory for US Marines)
Sept 1916 — Tanks are used for the first time	*30 June 1917* — Start of Third Battle of Ypres	*21 March–18 July 1918* — Germany's Spring Offensive on the Western Front ends in failure
29 April 1917 — First of over 100 mutinies in French Army	Germany signs an armistice with the Allies, bringing an end to the war — *11 Nov 1918*	

1917   **1918**   **1919**

☼ COMMUNISM ☼

During the nineteenth century, radical thinkers developed the idea of a classless society where everyone is equal. To achieve this vision, known as communism, the 'capitalist' system of private ownership and the free market would have to be overthrown in a revolution. During the twentieth century, various attempts were made at creating communist societies. These mostly resulted in brutal tyrannies with power concentrated in the hands of an individual or small group.

This propaganda poster from the Chinese Revolution shows Mao and his famous 'Little Red Book' of quotations from his speeches and writings. It became an inspirational text for millions of Chinese communists.

The Bolshevik Revolution was led by Vladimir Lenin.

China

In 1949, the Chinese Communist Party under Mao Zedong took control of China. In the 1950s, Mao's attempt at rapid industrial and agricultural development – the 'Great Leap Forward' – caused a famine in which millions died. In the 1960s, Mao launched the 'Cultural Revolution', encouraging students to denounce intellectuals and party officials. This violent purge caused chaos. In the 1970s, moderates won power, and China began a process of economic modernisation.

Soviet Union

In 1917, the communist Bolsheviks seized control of the Russian Empire and renamed it the Soviet Union. Stalin, the leader from 1924, embarked on a programme of rapid industrialisation. He ruthlessly reorganised the countryside, abolishing private land and creating enormous collective farms. This caused a terrible famine. Stalin's growing paranoia led to a great purge of party members. Millions were sent to labour camps called gulags.

Russian Revolution leads to the establishment of the Union of Soviet Socialist Republics (USSR), or Soviet Union **1917**

Vietnamese Revolution: a communist-dominated nationalist movement, the Viet Minh, overturn French colonial rule in Vietnam **1945**

Mongolian Revolution: with Soviet help, Mongolians founded the Mongolian People's Republic, which became a satellite state of the Soviet Union **1921**

Chinese Revolution: Chinese communists under Mao Zedong establish the People's Republic of China **1949**

German Revolution ends in defeat for the communists **1918–19**

Spanish Revolution, fought between Nationalists and Republicans (including communists) **1936**

1945 Creation of communist North Korea

The Khmer Rouge established a brutal communist regime in Cambodia.

Rest of Asia

Various communist groups, inspired and supported by either the Soviet Union or China, took power in their countries. These included Mongolia (1921), Vietnam (1945), Laos and Cambodia (both 1975). The Soviet Union installed a communist regime in North Korea in 1948. Failed communist revolutions and insurgencies (prolonged struggles) occurred in Indonesia, Malaya and the Philippines.

Latin America

Communist movements waged long and bloody struggles with regimes in Latin America. In Peru, the Shining Path was inspired by Mao. The FMLN of El Salvador followed the Russian revolutionary leader, Lenin. In Nicaragua, the Sandinistas took power in a 1979 revolution. The Cuban revolution (1953–9) brought to power a communist regime under Fidel Castro.

Castro and his followers fought a long guerrilla war against government forces before taking power in Cuba.

1959 Cuban Revolution: Revolutionaries under Fidel Castro seize power in Cuba

1964 Chairman Mao's 'Little Red Book' is first published

1979 Nicaraguan Revolution: The Sandanistas, a communist movement, establish a revolutionary government in Nicaragua

1975–9 A communist movement, the Khmer Rouge, led by Pol Pot, rule Cambodia

1974 Benin and Ethiopia become communist states

1991 Collapse of the Soviet Union

Somalia becomes a communist state **1969** **1970** Congo becomes a communist state **1989** Fall of the Berlin Wall

⚙ THE GREAT DEPRESSION ⚙

The 1920s was a time of great prosperity in the United States. It came to an abrupt end in October 1929 when the New York Stock Market on Wall Street (where company stocks are traded) crashed. Stock prices plummeted in a frenzy of panic selling. The Wall Street Crash caused banks and businesses to go bust. Many people were laid off work. The 'Great Depression', as it became known, spread from the USA to much of the rest of the world.

The Nazis were anti-Semitic, and introduced laws discriminating against Jews. All Jews were required to wear a yellow Star of David as a way of marking them out.

Soup kitchens opened to feed the poor.

USA

By 1933, some 13 million Americans were out of work. Many lost their homes, and soon shanty towns, known as Hoovervilles, began appearing on the outskirts of cities. They were named after US President Herbert Hoover, who was blamed by many for the Depression. Farmers lost their land due to sharp falls in income and a terrible drought on the Great Plains, known as the Dust Bowl. President Franklin Roosevelt launched a New Deal programme in 1933, getting Americans working again through big public works projects.

Germany

Of all the countries in Europe, Germany was hit hardest by the Great Depression. By 1932, unemployment had reached six million. Popular discontent led to the rise of extremist parties. In 1933, Adolf Hitler's Nazi Party gained power. The regime abolished democracy and took control of industry. Unemployment was eliminated through massive public works projects.

Wall Street Crash: share prices collapse on the New York Stock Exchange in October 1929 — **29 October 1929**

Banks and businesses close; unemployment soars; the world slides into depression — **1930**

Japanese troops march into Manchuria, September 1931.

Japan

Japan suffered a series of economic recessions in the 1920s, made worse by a devastating earthquake in 1923. The Great Depression struck Japan hard because of its reliance on foreign trade. Lacking land and natural resources, Japan invaded Manchuria in north-eastern China. Public opinion turned against the democratic government. In 1932, after the prime minister was assassinated, a military dictatorship took over.

Latin America

Latin America was hit badly by the Great Depression, as US and European demand for their coffee, beef, oil and cotton dropped. In some countries, including Brazil and Argentina, this led to the rise of fascist (undemocratic, nationalist, militaristic) governments, similar to those taking power in parts of Europe.

Getúlio Vargas, a fascist-style leader, took power in Brazil in 1930. He suppressed communism and tried to encourage industry by lowering taxes and raising import duties.

1934 The US economy slowly starts to recover. Sweden is the first country to fully recover from the Great Depression

March 1933 Franklin Delano Roosevelt becomes president of the USA. By this time, some 15 million Americans are unemployed and nearly half the country's banks have failed

1934–6 The Dust Bowl affects 388,500 sq km, including parts of Oklahoma, Kansas, Colorado, Texas and New Mexico

1941–5 The Holocaust: some six million European Jews are systematically murdered by the Nazis

1939–41 The Great Depression ends, helped by massive government spending during the Second World War

1935 .... 1940 1945

☼ THE SECOND WORLD WAR ☼

Germany's leader Adolf Hitler believed in the German people's right to conquer lands to the east for greater 'living space'. He began to take over territories, including Austria in 1938. Alarmed by German expansionism, Britain and France (the Allies) threatened war if Poland was invaded. In 1939, Germany invaded Poland, and the Second World War began.

Allied troops land on the Normandy Beaches on D-Day, 6 June 1944.

Europe

The Germans launched a blitzkrieg ('lightning war') – a terrifying assault using tanks and dive-bombers – against Western Europe, and by July 1940 most of the continent was under German control. Only Britain remained undefeated. In 1944 the Allies (including the USA, which entered the war in 1941) invaded occupied Europe in an operation called D-Day. Gradually, they drove the German forces back. Germany surrendered in May 1945.

Soviet Union

Germany and its allies (the Axis powers) invaded the Soviet Union in June 1941. The Axis made rapid progress, but instead of capturing Moscow, they pressed deeper on three fronts, and their forces became overstretched. The Axis forces launched fresh offensives in 1942, but by now the Soviets had mobilised a vast army. After the Axis suffered a devastating defeat at Stalingrad in January 1943, Soviet forces began driving them back.

Soviet soldier waves a banner at Stalingrad, one of the bloodiest battles in the history of warfare.

Germany invades Poland. The Second World War begins — *Sept 1939*

June 1940 — South Africa declares war on Italy

Indian National Congress refuses to help British war effort, leading to mass arrests of INC by British — *Aug 1942*

Italian forces invade Egypt from Libya — *Sept 1940*

June 1941 — Germany invades the Soviet Union

British India declares war on Germany — *Sept 1939*

Operation Torch: Allied landings in Morocco and Algeria — *Nov 1942*

Japan attacks Pearl Harbor — *Dec 1941*

North Africa

The Axis powers invaded North Africa to try to seize control of the Suez Canal and cut off British oil supplies from the Middle East. By May 1942, Axis forces were just 320 km from the canal, but in October a British army defeated them at El Alamein. By May 1943, Axis forces had been driven from North Africa.

Lieutenant-General Montgomery led British forces to victory at El Alamein, Egypt.

Japan finally surrendered in 1945 after the USA dropped atomic bombs on two of its cities.

Pacific

In 1941, the USA declared war on Japan after the Japanese attacked its fleet at Pearl Harbor. In a series of victories in early 1942, Japan conquered South-East Asia and came in striking range of Australia and India. The tide began to turn in June 1942, when the USA defeated the Japanese at Midway. Over the next three years, the Japanese were gradually pushed back across the Pacific.

Sept 1942–Jan 1943	Battle of Stalingrad ends in German defeat
19 April 1943	Warsaw Ghetto Uprising: Jews in Warsaw in German-occupied Poland resist Nazi efforts to transport them to death camp
Feb 1943	US take Guadalcanal after 6-month campaign
Allies invade Sicily *July 1943*	*Sept 1943* Italy surrenders

Japanese navy is destroyed at Battle of Leyte Gulf *Oct 1944*

British Indian Army *1945* numbers 2.5 million men

June 1944 D-Day landings

Mar 1945 Allied forces cross the Rhine

Aug 1945 Atomic bombs dropped on Hiroshima and Nagasaki

May 1945 Germany surrenders

Sept 1945 Japan surrenders. End of the Second World War

THE COLD WAR

After the Second World War, the Soviet Union installed pro-Soviet, communist governments in Eastern Europe. This expansionism angered the USA and its allies (the West), and their relations with the Soviet Union deteriorated. This marked the beginning of the Cold War – a state of non-violent conflict between the USA, the Soviet Union, and their respective allies, that would last for the next 45 years.

US helicopters protected South Vietnamese troops during the Vietnam War.

A parade through Moscow's Red Square, showing Soviet military might.

Soviet Union

In 1949, the Soviets tested an atomic bomb, sparking a nuclear arms race with the USA. In the 1970s there was a thaw in relations, which lasted until 1979, when the Soviet invasion of Afghanistan raised tensions again. In the 1980s, Soviet leader Gorbachev realised the Soviet Union could no longer compete with the USA economically and tried to end the Cold War. But his attempts at liberal reform unleashed forces he couldn't control. In 1991 the Soviet Union collapsed.

Asia

When communist North Korea invaded the South in 1950, a US-led force drove them out. But US attempts to topple the communists in the North led to confrontation with China. The war ended in stalemate. In the 1960s, the USA supported South Vietnam in its fight against the communist North. As the war became increasingly brutal, US public opinion turned against it. The USA withdrew in 1975. A year later, the communists captured the South.

1946 — Start of the Cold War. Churchill announces an 'iron curtain' has descended across Europe

1955 — The Warsaw Pact (a military alliance of communist states) is established

1956 — Hungarian uprising is crushed by Soviet forces

Oct 1962 — Cuban Missile Crisis

1948–9 — Berlin blockade: after Soviet troops blockade West Berlin, the West supplies Berliners with food and fuel by air

1961 — The Berlin Wall is built by the East German government, dividing the city in two and preventing East Germans from escaping to the more prosperous West

1949 — The Soviet Union tests its first atomic bomb; NATO (North Atlantic Treaty Organisation), a military alliance aimed at preventing further Soviet expansion in Europe, is established

The Cuban Missile Crisis (1962) brought the USA and Soviet Union to the brink of nuclear confrontation. It was depicted at the time as a battle of wills between the two leaders, US President John F Kennedy and Soviet Premier Nikita Khrushchev.

Americas

The spread of communism caused deep unease in the USA. In the 1950s, fears that communists had infiltrated the US government caused many to lose their jobs. In 1962, Soviet missile bases were discovered on Cuba, very nearly sparking all-out war between the USA and the Soviet Union. The USA tried to influence Latin American politics, backing anti-communist groups, and taking action against communist regimes in places such as Bolivia, Guatemala, Cuba and Chile.

Europe

Eastern Europe lay on the front line of the Cold War. Communist East Germany built a wall through divided Berlin to prevent the people in the east of the city fleeing to the more liberal west. Uprisings pushing for more freedom in Hungary (1956) and Czechoslovakia (1968) provoked brutal crackdowns. In 1989 Gorbachev's liberal policies led to the opening of east-west borders in Eastern Europe. The Berlin Wall fell, and communist governments swiftly collapsed. The Cold War was over.

The fall of the Berlin Wall – hated symbol of the Cold War.

Berlin Wall is dismantled; end of the Cold War 1989

1968 Warsaw Pact forces crush Czechoslovakian uprising

Collapse of the Soviet Union 1991

⚙ DECOLONISATION ⚙

The First World War left the colonial powers severely weakened and less able to enforce their rule overseas. This encouraged indigenous peoples in the colonies to push for independence. In some cases, such as Libya and the Philippines, independence was granted without much struggle. In other places, such as India, Vietnam, Algeria and Kenya, it arose only after a fight.

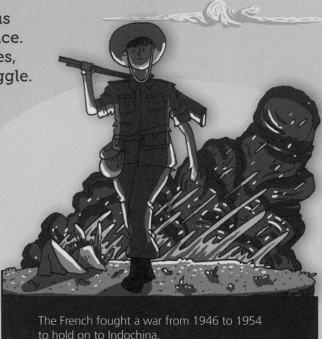

The French fought a war from 1946 to 1954 to hold on to Indochina.

In 1930, Gandhi led thousands on the 'salt march' to the sea to protest against a salt tax.

India

During the early twentieth century, the Indian National Congress (an organisation campaigning for independence from Britain) became a mass movement. Under the leadership of Mohandas Gandhi, the Congress organised non-violent protests, including strikes, demonstrations and boycotts of British goods. Independence was finally granted in 1947. Amid great violence, the country was partitioned between Hindu India and Muslim Pakistan.

South-East Asia

During their occupation of territories in this region in the Second World War, the Japanese promised liberation from colonial rule. This stoked the flames of nationalism, and after the war the colonial powers struggled to reimpose their authority. The British agreed to withdraw from Burma and, after a struggle with communist guerrillas, from Malaya. The Netherlands granted independence to the Dutch East Indies.

Philippines wins political independence from the USA, although the USA retains dozens of military bases and maintains some economic control over the island nation — 1946

Burma wins independence from Britain following the signing of the Panglong Agreement — 1948

India wins independence from Britain, and is partitioned into two countries, India (with a Hindu majority) and Pakistan (predominantly Muslim) — 1947

Indonesia wins independence from the Netherlands after four years of guerilla warfare — 1950

Africa

After the Second World War, an emerging class of educated Africans led calls for independence. The former Italian colony of Libya was the first to achieve this, in 1951. The French gave up Algeria after an eight-year war. By 1965, almost all African colonies had achieved independence. Yet a white minority clung to power in Rhodesia until 1980 when it became Zimbabwe, and in South Africa until a multiracial democracy was achieved in 1994 under the leadership of Nelson Mandela.

In South Africa, Nelson Mandela, imprisoned in 1964 as an activist for the African National Congress (ANC), was released in 1990 and became the country's first democratically elected president in 1994.

Middle East

When the Ottoman Empire collapsed following the First World War, its former territories were divided between the European powers. Britain took control of Egypt, Iraq, Palestine and several smaller states; France gained Syria and Lebanon. Nationalist uprisings led to independence for Egypt (1922), Iraq (1932), Lebanon (1943) and Syria (1946). British authority in Palestine ended in 1948, after which it became the Jewish state of Israel (see page 19).

Egyptian nationalists protest against British rule in 1919.

 1961 Wars of liberation in Portuguese African colonies begin

Jamaica, and Trinidad and Tobago win independence from UK **1962** **1966** Guyana and Barbados win independence from UK

1983 By this date, Bahamas, Grenada, Dominica, Saint Lucia, St Vincent and the Grenadines, Antigua and Barbuda, Belize, Saint Kitts and Nevis have gained independence from UK

1963 Kenya wins independence from Britain following the nationalist Mau-Mau Uprising

 1962 Algeria wins independence from France after a bitter eight-year war

☼ THE MIDDLE EAST IN CONFLICT ☼

The discovery of crude oil in the Middle East brought wealth to the ruling elites, and led Western governments, who relied on this oil, to try to exert political influence in the region. Many in the region saw this as a new form of colonialism. In the 1950s, anti-Western, nationalist regimes swept to power in Egypt, Syria and Iraq. But they failed to bring prosperity and became increasingly despotic.

Explosion from a car bomb attack by ISIS in Syrian city of Kobani.

Saddam Hussein's statue is toppled following the 2003 invasion of Iraq.

Iraq

Iraq, under Saddam Hussein, invaded Iran in 1980, sparking an eight-year war. In 1990, Saddam invaded Kuwait, but was driven out by a US-led force. Saddam was deposed in a US-led invasion in 2003, ushering in a period of chaos and civil war. ISIS, a violent Islamist group, took advantage of the turmoil to seize large parts of the country in 2014.

Syria

The regime of Bashar al-Assad routinely tortured and killed political opponents. When protests broke out in 2011, Assad sent in his army, and the country quickly descended into civil war. ISIS joined the rebellion, managing to capture large swathes of Syria. Russia gave military support to Assad, while the West fought back against ISIS.

1905 Founding of conservative Salafiyyah movement within Sunni Islam

1928 Ḥasan al-Bannāʾ founds the Muslim Brotherhood, dedicated to Islamist reform in Egypt

General Islam Conference held in Jerusalem *1931*

League of Arab States founded in Cairo, Egypt *1945*

1906 Founding of All-India Muslim League, supporting establishment of a separate Muslim-majority state of Pakistan

Egypt gains independence from UK *1922*

1932 Iraq gains independence

1941 Abū al-Aʿlā Maududi founds Jamaʿat-i Islami, the Muslim Brotherhood equivalent in South Asia

1922 Turkish nationalists seize control of Turkey and abolish the 600-year-old Ottoman Empire

Iran

Islamism, a conservative political movement within Islam, first came to the world's attention in 1979, when Islamists took power in Iran. The Islamic Republic of Iran, as it became, was hostile to the West, especially the USA. The regime sponsored Islamist groups in neighbouring Lebanon and, later, Iraq.

Iranians hold aloft a picture of their new leader Ayatollah Khomeini during the revolution in 1979.

Israel/Palestine

Since Palestine became the Jewish state of Israel in 1948, it has been fought over by Jews and Palestinians (the Arab Muslim inhabitants of the territory). Israel fought numerous defensive wars against neighbouring Arab states, and confronted two major uprisings by Palestinian groups in the disputed territories of the West Bank and Gaza Strip. A peace process began in the 1990s, yet the conflict has rumbled on into the twenty-first century, with no end in sight.

Palestinian fighters during the second intifadah (uprising), 2000–2005.

 1967 Six Day War: Israel defeats Arab neighbours and greatly expands its territory

Islamist train bombings kill 192 in Madrid **11 March 2004**

Islamist terror attacks in Paris **2015** kill 137

 1956 Suez Crisis: Israel, France and Britain launch joint attack on Egypt after Egypt takes control of Suez Canal

1979 The Iranian Revolution

Iran-Iraq War **1980–1988**

US-led invasion of Iraq **2003**

Islamist terrorists set off bombs on Indonesian island of Bali, killing 202 **12 October 2002**

Islamist suicide bomber attacks a pop concert in **2017** Manchester, UK

Islamist terrorists attack targets in the USA, killing 2,996 **11 September 2001**

7 July 2005 Islamist bombings in London kill 53

⚙ HEALTH AND DISEASE ⚙

Since 1900, there have been remarkable improvements in physical health, thanks to better diet and medicine. Landmark advances include the development of antibiotics to cure bacterial diseases, vaccines to cure viral diseases, organ transplantation, and 3-D scans of the body's interior. As people travelled more widely, diseases spread across continents. The 1918 influenza pandemic was the most deadly in history, killing 50–100 million.

A polio epidemic in 1952 spurred the development of Salk's vaccine. Salk tested the vaccine on himself, his wife and his three sons.

Scottish scientist Sir Alexander Fleming discovered penicillin by accident as the mould growing on a petri dish.

USA

With the invention of more powerful microscopes in the 1940s, biologists could start to study viruses. This enabled American doctor Jonas Salk to develop a vaccine for polio. In 1953, the anaesthesiologist Virginia Apgar introduced the Apgar score to assess the health of newborn babies. In the 1960s and '70s, Maurice Hilleman developed vaccines for measles, mumps, rubella, chickenpox, bacterial meningitis and hepatitis B.

Europe

In 1901 an Austrian, Karl Landsteiner, classified the main blood groups, enabling doctors to safely transfuse blood. A few years later, Frederick Hopkins and Casimir Funk discovered vitamins. The first antibacterial drugs were developed by German scientists Paul Ehrlich and Gerhard Domagk for treating diseases such as syphilis, pneumonia and meningitis.

 1900 British physiologists Starling and Bayliss discover the first hormone

 1928 Scottish biologist Sir Alexander Fleming discovers penicillin, paving the way for the development of antibiotics

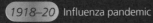 **1918–20** Influenza pandemic

American surgeon revolutionises heart surgery with **1953** his invention of the heart-lung machine

x

Vera Gedroitz (1870–1932) was Russia's first female surgeon.

Russia

In the 1920s, psychologist Bluma Zeigarnik discovered that incomplete tasks are easier to remember than successful ones – this is known as the Zeigarnik effect. Nikolai Korotkov pioneered vascular (blood vessel) surgery and invented a new technique for measuring blood pressure. In 1930, Soviet surgeons Vladimir Shamov and Sergei Yudin performed the first blood transfusions from recently deceased donors, and Yudin set up the world's first blood bank. Later that decade, surgeons Yuri Voronoy and Vladimir Demikhov attempted the first organ transplants.

Africa

Since the 1900s, many new diseases have emerged that originated in the tropical forests of Africa. These include HIV/AIDS, Ebola, the Marburg virus, Hantavirus, Lyme disease, Lassa fever and Rift Valley fever. This may have happened because human populations expanded into these previously uninhabited areas. Diseases afflicting forest animals then crossed species into humans.

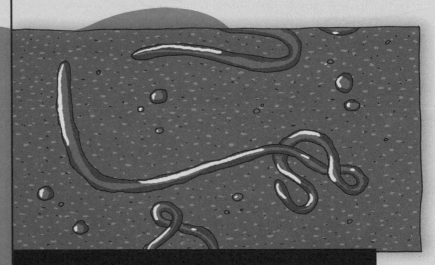

A view through a microscope of the Ebola virus. An outbreak of Ebola in West Africa (2013–16) killed over 11,000 people.

 1967 South African surgeon Christiaan Barnard carries out first successful heart transplant

 First remote surgical operation carried out by surgeons in New York, USA, on a **2001** patient in Strasbourg, France

 1978 Smallpox is eradicated. The world's first test-tube baby, Louise Brown, is born in the UK

First full face transplant **2010** is carried out in Spain

English electrical engineer Godfrey **1973** Hounsfield invents the CAT scanner

 1981 HIV/AIDS becomes a worldwide pandemic

Scientists in Japan are the first to grow a **2013** human liver from stem cells

⚙ ENVIRONMENTAL CHALLENGES ⚙

The surge in industrialisation that began in the early 1800s has had a serious impact on the Earth's environment. Visible effects include air and water pollution, the expansion of deserts, deforestation and the extinction of species. Potentially the most serious long-term impact is global warming, or the greenhouse effect. Since 1970, increasing efforts have been made to protect the environment. International agreements have been reached to reduce the emission of greenhouse gases such as carbon dioxide.

USA

Some of the world's first environmentalists were Americans, including Gifford Pinchot, John Muir and Aldo Leopold, who promoted nature conservation. Rachel Carson's 1962 book *Silent Spring*, describing the damage of the insecticide DDT, helped launch the modern environmental movement. Yet today the USA remains one of the world's major polluters. In 2014, it emitted 16.5 tonnes of carbon dioxide per person.

US president Theodore Roosevelt (right) with John Muir, founder of the Sierra Club, one of the world's first environmental groups.

Arctic sea ice melts earlier each year, making it harder for polar bears to hunt seals.

Arctic

The effects of global warming have been most noticeable in the Arctic. Rising temperatures have caused a loss of sea ice and the melting of the Greenland ice sheet. This has threatened species such as polar bears, turtles and right whales. It also threatens the release of the greenhouse gas methane, currently trapped beneath the permafrost (frozen ground).

1909 US President Theodore Roosevelt organises the North American Conservation Conference

1916 US President Woodrow Wilson founds the National Park Service

1919 Forestry Commission established in Britain to increase the amount of woodland

World Conservation Union is founded 1948

A highly influential book on conservation, *A Sandy County Almanac,* by Aldo Leopold, is published 1948

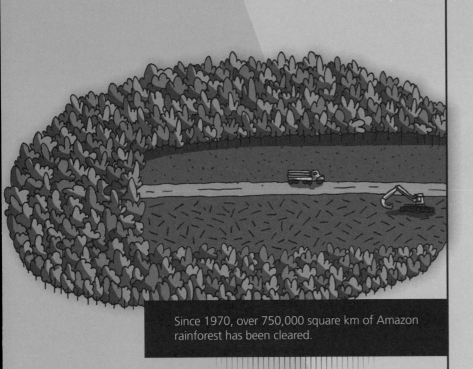

Since 1970, over 750,000 square km of Amazon rainforest has been cleared.

South America

The Amazon rainforest covers over 5.2 million square km. Ten per cent of the world's species live there, its plants have uses as medicines, and it is home to many indigenous communities. It also has the highest rate of deforestation. People cut down its trees for timber, cattle ranching and crop farming. Since 2004, the rate of deforestation has slowed, but the rainforest continues to shrink.

China

China's rapid industrialisation since the 1970s has come at a huge environmental cost. Since 2007, it has been the world's biggest emitter of greenhouse gases. It also suffers from severe water and air pollution in many of its cities. Air pollution alone contributes to an estimated 1.2 million premature deaths each year. The situation has caused growing social unrest. In 2013, the government began taking action to reduce emissions.

Smog in Beijing in January 2013. Roads and schools were closed and flights were cancelled.

Millions gather in USA for first Earth Day 1970

International Whaling 1982 Commission bans all commercial whaling

EU commits to cutting greenhouse gas emissions 2007 by 20 per cent by 2020

2017 USA withdraws from Paris Agreement

International agreement to ban 1987 substances that damage the ozone layer

California is first US state to cap 2006 greenhouse gas emissions

Greenpeace, the environmental 1971 pressure group, is founded

Kyoto Protocol, an international agreement to reduce greenhouse gas 1997 emissions, is negotiated

Paris Agreement to reduce greenhouse gas emissions 2016 signed by 194 Parties

1960 .... 1970 .... 1980 .... 1990 .... 2000 2010

⚙ SCIENCE AND TECHNOLOGY ⚙

The years since 1900 have witnessed spectacular achievements in science and technology. Thousands of scientists have engaged in ever more specialised fields, while governments and corporations have spent vast sums on research. The development of email and the Internet has made it possible for scientists to exchange information quickly and easily.

In 1996, a team at the Roslin Institute in Scotland cloned the first mammal from an adult body cell – a sheep called Dolly.

In 2013, the LHC proved the existence of a new particle, the Higgs boson.

Britain

Britain led the way in a number of technologies: John Logie Baird invented the first working television system; Robert Watson-Watt developed radar; and Tim Berners-Lee invented the World Wide Web. At Cambridge University, molecular biologists James Watson and Francis Crick, with help from chemist Rosalind Franklin, explained the structure of DNA, the carrier of genetic information.

Europe

German physicist Albert Einstein transformed physics with his Special and General Theories of Relativity, showing that space and time are relative, and gravity is a distortion in space-time. In the 1920s Heisenberg and Schrödinger developed quantum theory, explaining the physics of the sub-atomic world. The Large Hadron Collider (LHC) was built in the 2000s to test unsolved questions in physics.

1903 — American inventors the Wright brothers achieve powered flight

1905 — Albert Einstein proposes his Special Theory of Relativity

American inventor Lee de Forest develops the vacuum tube — 1906

1913 — Danish physicist Niels Bohr explains the structure of the atom

Scottish scientist Robert Watson-Watt develops radar — 1935

American astronomer Edwin Hubble discovers the nature of galaxies and the expansion of the universe — 1929

US scientists John Bardeen, William Shockley and Walter Brattain develop the transistor — 1947

1942–45 — A team of US scientists develop the atomic bomb

USA

The Wright brothers invented the first heavier-than-air flying machine. Lee de Forest's vacuum tube – a key component of early radio, radar, TV and computer systems – was later replaced by the transistor, another US invention. ARPANET, a forerunner of the Internet, was created in the 1960s. NASA scientists sent rockets and probes into space and landed the first humans on the Moon.

In the 2000s, US company Google began developing a driverless car.

Soviet Union

In the 1940s, Igor Sikorsky built the Sikorsky R-4, the world's first mass-produced helicopter. The first nuclear power plant was built at Obninsk in 1954. Sputnik 1, the first artificial satellite, was launched in 1957. Two years later, Luna 1 became the first spacecraft to escape Earth orbit. And in 1961, Yuri Gagarin became the first human in space.

Gagarin completed one orbit of Earth in his spacecraft, Vostok 1.

1953 British-based scientists Watson and Crick describe DNA

1957 The Soviet Union launches Sputnik 1

1961 Soviet cosmonaut Yuri Gagarin becomes the first human in space

1969 American astronaut Neil Armstrong sets foot on the Moon

1981 US technology company IBM launches the first personal computer, or PC

1990 NASA launches the Hubble Space Telescope

2014 Philae lander, released by Rosetta space probe, is the first spacecraft to make a soft landing on a comet

2012 Voyager 1 becomes the first spacecraft to cross into interstellar space

1960 ·········· 1970 ·········· 1980 ·········· 1990 ·········· 2000 ·········· 2010

⚙ ART ⚙

Modern art began in the latter half of the nineteenth century and continued until the 1970s. It was a period in which artists cast aside tradition and began experimenting with new styles. Art moved away from the figurative (representing things as they look) and towards the abstract (achieving effects through shapes, colours and textures).

Grant Wood used his sister and his dentist as the models for the couple depicted in his famous painting, *American Gothic*.

Picasso's *Three Musicians* is a Cubist painting that's a little like an intricate puzzle made of pieces of cut-out paper.

Europe

Art movements that flowered in the early twentieth century included Fauvism, Cubism, Expressionism, Futurism, Dadaism and Surrealism. Among the most influential artists of this time were Pablo Picasso, Henri Matisse and Marcel Duchamp. The 1990s saw the rise to prominence of the 'Young British Artists', including Damien Hirst and Tracey Emin.

USA

Artists such as John Marin and Georgia O'Keeffe painted in modernist styles. Later, Grant Wood and Edward Hopper produced figurative paintings of urban and rural America. After the Second World War, New York artists Jackson Pollock and Mark Rothko achieved international acclaim with a new style: Abstract Expressionism. In the 1960s, Pop artist Andy Warhol reproduced everyday objects from popular culture.

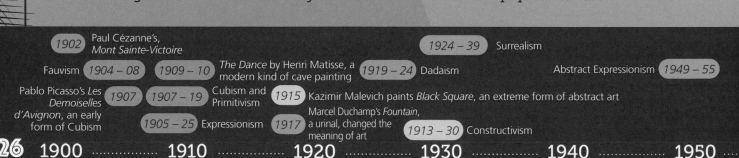

1902 Paul Cézanne's, *Mont Sainte-Victoire*

1924 – 39 Surrealism

Fauvism *1904 – 08*   *1909 – 10* *The Dance* by Henri Matisse, a modern kind of cave painting

1919 – 24 Dadaism

Abstract Expressionism *1949 – 55*

Pablo Picasso's *Les Demoiselles d'Avignon*, an early form of Cubism   *1907*   *1907 – 19* Cubism and Primitivism   *1915* Kazimir Malevich paints *Black Square*, an extreme form of abstract art

1905 – 25 Expressionism   *1917* Marcel Duchamp's *Fountain*, a urinal, changed the meaning of art

1913 – 30 Constructivism

Soviet Union

The constructivist art movement, which used mechanical objects to create abstract structural forms, was founded in Russia in 1913, and became a dominant art style in the early Soviet Union. It was officially replaced in 1934 by Socialist Realism. This style was always figurative (not abstract). It showed everyday scenes in the Soviet Union, yet always in a positive and optimistic light. It romanticised the lives of common workers, be they in factories or on farms, and never showed tragedy or unhappiness. Its purpose was to show Soviet citizens how they could and should be.

A socialist realist painting showing revolutionary leader Lenin with villagers.

A mural by Diego Rivera showing the Aztec city of Tenochtitlan.

Latin America

The art of Latin America was greatly influenced by a Russian movement called Constructivism – combining mechanical objects to form abstract artworks. Another home-grown movement was Muralism – the painting of large murals (wall paintings) with nationalist political messages – which started in Mexico in the wake of the revolution. In the 1920s, Mexican artist Frida Kahlo began painting scenes from traditional Mexican culture in a surrealist style.

1970s onwards Graffiti artists use aerosol spray cans and stencils to create urban street art	**1989** Neo-Pop artists such as Jeff Koons use the icons of popular culture to make art
c. 1922 – 69 Socialist Realism	Projection artists project their art onto different kinds of surfaces, including buildings **2000s**
Video Art **1972 – 94**	**1954 – 85** Pop Art **1990s** Body Art – artists' own bodies become their canvas
1920s –70s Muralism Young British Artists start to exhibit together in London **1988**	**1999** Stuckists favour a return to figurative painting

GLOBALISATION

Since the European age of exploration in the fifteenth and sixteenth centuries, the world has been growing ever more interconnected. This process of globalisation accelerated in the late twentieth and early twenty-first centuries due to the lowering of trade barriers, the fall of communism, cheaper transportation and technological advances such as the Internet. Increasingly, nations acted together to confront challenges such as climate change, pandemics, the drug trade and terrorism.

Europe

In the 1950s, several European countries formed a trading bloc called the EEC. In time, the EEC became the European Union (EU). A central bank was established, and a common currency, the euro. When a global recession struck in 2008, the EU's principle of free movement of people began causing tensions. Populist parties demanded more control over immigration. In 2016 the UK, a member since 1973, voted in a referendum to leave the EU.

In 2016 Donald Trump, a billionaire and reality television star, rode a wave of popular discontent to be elected US president.

USA

In 2007–8, a crisis in the banking sector led to the worst recession since 1945 and posed a major challenge to globalisation. Despite government efforts to stimulate the economy, the recovery was patchy, and wages remained stagnant. Many blamed out-of-touch politicians, Wall Street banks, globalisation and immigration for their problems.

The Maastricht Treaty, signed in 1993, created the European Union.

Creation of the World Bank and a general agreement on international rules for tariffs and trade — 1944

Founding of the United Nations to promote international peace and cooperation — 1945

China

China has benefited more than any other country from globalisation. Between 1980 and 2010, its economy grew by an average of 10 per cent a year. It is now the world's leading exporter of goods and the second biggest economy after the USA. Yet rapid economic expansion has caused social problems. Growing inequality between rich and poor has stoked anger and sometimes violent unrest in poorer, rural communities.

China's growth fuelled a building boom in its cities.

Africa

Globalisation has both benefited and damaged Africa. More countries are investing in Africa, creating jobs and infrastructure. Yet the wealth generated by this investment doesn't always benefit local communities. Also, globalisation has led to a 'brain drain' in many African countries, as skilled and educated people have migrated to places like Europe and North America.

Mobile devices and Internet access have brought people in many parts of the world closer together.

The creation of the World Wide Web enables instant communication around the globe — **1991**

2007 – 8 Banking crisis leads to global recession

The end of the Cold War leaves capitalism as the single dominant economic system — **1989**

1994 The North American Free Trade Agreement takes effect

1958 Six European countries form the EEC

The creation of the European Union strengthens economic and political ties between the European nations — **1993**

1995 World Trade Organisation is created to help free trade

GLOSSARY

antibiotic
A medicine such as penicillin that destroys or prevents the growth of microorganisms.

armistice
An agreement made by opposing sides in a war to stop fighting for a certain time.

artillery
Heavy guns used in land warfare.

atomic bomb
A bomb that gets its destructive power from the rapid release of nuclear energy through the splitting of atoms in a chain reaction.

bacterial
To do with bacteria, a type of microorganism.

blockade
Seal off (a place) to prevent goods or people from entering or leaving.

boycott
A refusal to buy or handle (goods) as a punishment or protest.

capitalist
Describing an economic system in which a country's trade and industry are controlled by private individuals for profit, rather than by the state.

CAT scanner
A device used in medicine for displaying a cross-section through the human body using computer-controlled X-rays.

clone
Produce an organism that is genetically identical to another organism.

Cold War
The state of hostility that existed between the Soviet Union, the United States, and their respective allies between 1945 and 1989.

colony
A country or territory under the political control of another country and occupied by settlers from that country.

communist
Describing a country in which a single party controls property, trade and production with the stated aim of creating an equal society.

deforestation
The clearance of forest or trees (from an area).

democracy
A system of government under which the leaders have been elected freely by all the citizens.

despotic
Describing a government that holds absolute power and typically exercises it in a cruel or oppressive way.

DNA
The molecule, present in all living organisms, that carries its genetic information.

genetic
Relating to genes, a basic unit consisting of a sequence of DNA that transmits characteristics from one generation to the next.

greenhouse effect
The trapping of the Sun's warmth in Earth's lower atmosphere due to an increasing quantity of certain gases in the atmosphere.

greenhouse gas
A gas that contributes to the greenhouse effect, such as carbon dioxide, caused by burning fossil fuels, and methane, caused by livestock farming.

guerrilla
A member of a small independent group typically fighting against larger regular forces.

heart-lung machine
A machine that temporarily takes over the function of the heart and lungs during surgery.

hormone
A substance produced by the body to stimulate specific cells or tissues into action.

indigenous
Native.

industrialisation
The large-scale development of industries (in a country or region).

Islamist
Someone who believes that public and political life should be guided by Islamic principles. It can also refer to someone who is prepared to use violent tactics in order to bring about an Islamic state.

mobilise
Assemble and prepare (troops) for war duty.

multiracial
Made up of or relating to people of more than one race or ethnicity.

nationalist
Describing a movement that believes in the right of its people to exist as a nation.

organ transplantation
A form of surgery in which a healthy organ is implanted in someone's body as a replacement for an unhealthy one.

pandemic
A rapid outbreak (of a disease) across a whole country or the world.

partition
Division (of a country) into separate nations.

propaganda
Information, typically of a biased and misleading nature, used to promote a political cause or regime.

quantum theory
A theory of matter and energy, based on the concept of quanta (discrete packages of energy).

radar
A system for detecting the presence, direction, distance and speed of approaching aircraft, ships or other objects. It works by sending out pulses of radio waves that are reflected off the object back to the source.

romanticise
Describe in an idealised or unrealistic fashion; make (something) seem better or more appealing than it is.

satellite
An artificial body placed in orbit around the Earth; or a country that is politically dependent on and supportive of another.

shanty town
A deprived area on the outskirts of a town consisting of a large number of shanties (small, crudely built dwellings).

smog
Fog or haze caused or made worse by air pollution.

stem cell A cell from an organism that can form into more cells of the same type.

stock
Also known as a share, this is one of the many equal parts into which ownership of a company is divided. The stocks of a company can be bought and sold on the stock market.

tariff
A tax to be paid on imports or exports (goods or services bought from or sold to a foreign country).

telecommunications
Communication over a distance by cable, telegraph, telephone or broadcasting.

test-tube baby
A baby conceived by in vitro fertilization (fertilization taking place in a test tube or elsewhere outside the womb).

trading bloc
A group of countries that have signed an agreement to reduce or eliminate barriers to trade.

transfuse
Transfer (blood) from one person to another.

vaccine
A substance that gives immunity to a disease.

virus
A type of microorganism that can only reproduce inside a host cell.

FURTHER INFORMATION

Books

Climate Change (Can the Earth Cope?)
Richard Spilsbury
Wayland, 2012

Communism (Systems of Government)
Sean Connolly
Franklin Watts, 2017

The Great Depression (Did Anything Good Come Out of)
Emma Marriott
Wayland, 2018

The Holocaust (Inquire and Investigate)
Tom Casteel and Carla Mooney
Nomad Press, 2017

The Horror of World War II (Deadly History)
Nancy Dickmann
Heinemann Educational, 2017

Nelson Mandela: Fighting to Dismantle Apartheid (Rebels with a Cause)
Ann Malaspina
Enslow, 2017

The Space Race: How the Cold War Put Humans on the Moon (Inquire and Investigate)
Matthew Brenden Wood
Nomad Press, 2018

You Wouldn't Want to be in the Trenches in World War I
Alex Woolf
Book House, 2014

Websites

You can find links to different topics within modern history here:
kids.kiddle.co/#Modern

Find information and resources on the World Wars here:
www.bbc.co.uk/history/worldwars/

Discover all the about Space Race here:
www.history.com/topics/space-race

Explore the history of the Cold War here:
www.ducksters.com/history/cold_war/summary.php

Learn about the formation of an independent India and Pakistan through a series of animated maps: **www.the-map-as-history.com/demos/tome11/04_independence_india_pakistan.php**

Learn about the history of modern China here:
www.bbc.co.uk/education/guides/zgtg87h/revision

INDEX